How children
what they learn

How children remember
what they learn in school

Graham Nuthall

NEW ZEALAND COUNCIL FOR EDUCATIONAL RESEARCH
WELLINGTON, 2000

NEW ZEALAND COUNCIL FOR EDUCATIONAL RESEARCH
PO Box 3237, Wellington, New Zealand

ISBN 1-877140-78-3

Distributed by NZCER Distribution Services
PO Box 3237, Wellington, New Zealand

Contents

1. Introduction 1
2. What we know about memory 3
3. The design of the research studies 9
4. The role of a working memory 14
5. What do pupils remember? 16
6. How do pupils forget? 19
7. Reconstructing and replacing
    forgotten information 22
8. Memory for classroom activities 29
9. The structure of knowledge in memory 33
10. Acquiring a memory: Piaget and Vygotsky 40
11. Activities that shape memory in the classroom 43
12. What this means for teaching 49

Further reading 55

References 56

Acknowledgements

The funding for the research described in this booklet was provided primarily by the New Zealand Ministry of Education, with additional funding from the University of Canterbury. Professor Adrienne Alton-Lee co-directed the project, and the original design of these studies was developed in her PhD thesis. Roger Corbett designed and operated the recording equipment. Greta Bowron, Anthea Clibborn-Brown and Kerry Hancock dedicated many hours to transcribing, coding, and analysing the data, and to helping us with the classroom observations and recordings.

1. Introduction

Understanding how memory works is critical to understanding how children learn. Memory creates the bridge between successive experiences, making it possible to learn by connecting current experiences with previous ones. Without memory, minds as we understand them could not exist. As Katherine Nelson puts it:

> *Memory is the primary form of all mental representations. Other forms such as concepts, categories, schema, imagination, dreams, pretence, plans, conjectures, stories, even language all derive from memory in some way. (Nelson, 1996, p.152)*

If memory were just the way we store experience, then it would not be an issue. But memory changes experience, and the way it makes these changes shapes the way we learn from experience. What we recall is a reconstruction of the original experience, based on a constantly changing version of that experience. For this reason, we cannot take memory for granted. If we are to understand how children learn from their classroom experiences, we need to understand how their memories interpret and shape those experiences.

This booklet is made up of three parts. The first part (sections 2 – 4) is about the background to our research. It describes what is already known about children's memory and how we went about studying the way children remember their classroom experiences and learning.

The second part of the booklet (sections 5 – 9) describes our results. It is about how children remember and forget what they learn in school. How do children remember the activities that make up their classroom life and how does their memory for classroom activities interact with, and shape, their memory for the curriculum content?

The third part of the booklet (sections 10 – 12) takes the analysis further. It deals first with the way classroom activities shape the development of children's memory. It is common these days to talk about Vygotsky and his theory of how children's minds are created through their social experiences. If Vygotsky's theory is right, then school experience is not just about acquiring knowledge and skills, but is also about shaping the fundamental processes that make up our minds. This is particularly true of the ways our minds interpret and store experience. In this part I look at how classroom activities shape children's memories and at how teachers can manage children's experiences in ways that will improve their ability to remember and use what they remember.

2. What we know about memory

The study of memory in adults and children goes back at least as far as the ancient Greeks. The history of modern experimental psychology begins with studies of people's ability to recall what they have learned. In those early experimental studies, the researchers tried to reduce the process of remembering to its essential or smallest components. In the interests of scientific precision, memory tasks were reduced to recalling lists of letters, numbers, and nonsense syllables. Memory was seen as a kind of storehouse in which pieces of information were stored as separate bits. Measures of memory were measures of how many bits you could recall.

In some ways, these early studies were useful for teachers. In a curriculum that emphasised the rote learning of number facts, historical dates, and texts, teachers could learn a lot from studies of memory for lists of letters, numbers or nonsense syllables. It mattered how many times you needed to rehearse a list, or whether you should spread your memorising over several days.

However, the curriculum has changed, and we are now more interested in the way children understand complex concepts and acquire general problem-solving skills. What we need to know is how memory affects this kind of learning. How, for example, do children recall their prior knowledge when they need it to solve a new problem? How do they remember previous problems and relate them to new problems, so that they see what the problems have in common? These questions require different kinds of answers from those supplied by previous research on memory.

Recent research on memory has focused more on how we remember the events in our daily lives and our distant past. We know, for example, how court witnesses remember the details of a significant event; how memory for traumatic personal experiences may, or may not, be repressed; and how memory for our past life changes with time. There have also been advances in our understanding of how we remember the stories we hear and the texts we read. Although only indirectly relevant, this research provides a basis for understanding how children remember what they experience and learn in the classroom.

Research on memory development in the preschool years has shown that it is closely related to the way children participate with adults in remembering activities (Fivush, 1991; Fivush, Haden & Adam, 1995; Hudson, 1990). Through their conversations with adults, young children gradually learn how to talk about past events and experiences. This learning occurs when parents talk with their children about family events such as picnics and visits to friends' homes, encouraging them to recall what happened and modelling for them the ways we talk about the past. Looking at photographs is often the occasion for such talk, with the photographs serving as cues for remembering and verifying and correcting what is recalled. Looking for lost objects is another occasion when memory may become the focus of parent-child talk.

According to Nelson (1993), these experiences give social significance to memories and remembering activities. Because of the way such talk is internalised, its sequential structure ("What happened? What happened next? What were we doing?", and so on) provides children with a structure for organising their experiences in memory.

There is also evidence that going to school shapes memory development (Sharp, Cole, & Lave, 1979). Several studies suggest that there is a major change in the way children remember experiences between the ages of five and seven years. In a series of studies comparing children who had attended the first year of formal schooling with others of the same age who had attended kindergarten, Morrison found that school experience changes the way children carry out memory tasks (Morrison, Smith, & Dow-Ehrensberger, 1995). Children who have been to school have better organised memories and more systematic ways of recalling past experiences. For many children, school may be the first time they have been asked to recall things that have no personal significance for them. Unlike parents talking to their children about family photographs, teachers ask children to recall facts that have no close connections to their personal and social lives.

In the first years of school, children have to learn ways of memorising information and recalling it when the teacher asks. For example, children need to learn how to judge when they have learned something sufficiently well to meet the demands of the classroom. Typically, if four-year-olds are asked to memorise something like the names of children at a party, they have little idea of what to do, and even less idea of when they know it sufficiently well to recall it. The six-year-old has a much better idea of what to do and a much more accurate sense of when something has been learned sufficiently well (Kreutzer, Leonard, & Flavell, 1975).

The organisation of memory
In order to understand how we remember the events and experiences of our everyday lives, we need to understand the way our memories are organised. It is the organisation of experience in memory that determines what is remembered and what is forgotten. Recent research,

especially that on recalling stories and past events, has made use of the concept of "schema", which refers to the way we structure our perceptions and understandings of the world. We have a schema for what we do when we go shopping at the supermarket. We have a schema for the way we ride a bicycle, for the typical plot of stories, for what we habitually do when we are angry, and so on. A schema consists of the underlying organisation of events and objects that make up a typical pattern of behaviour. It is something we acquire from repeated experiences, in which the details get forgotten and the repeated elements get remembered as a typical pattern or sequence. A schema is also referred to as a "script", by analogy with the script of a play.

When knowledge is stored in long-term memory, it is organised in nested hierarchies of schemata. Those at the top of a hierarchy are more abstract and generic (or schematic); those at the bottom are more specific, concrete, and detailed (Neisser, 1989). For example, our schema for shopping at a supermarket is nested within our more abstract schema for shopping in general. Each of the components that make up our schema for shopping at a supermarket is also organised as a schema, so that we have specific schemata for finding a parking space, for selecting objects from the shelves, for paying at the check-out, and so on.

As we go through the process of understanding a new experience, a representation of that experience is created and stored within the schema (or schemata) we use to understand the experience. This is what is meant when we say we understand new experiences by connecting them with our past experiences. With the passage of time the specific details of the experience are progressively lost, and the representation of the experience is gradually re-absorbed or integrated back into the organising schema.

Remembering a past experience involves relocating the schema (or schemata) where the representation of the experience is stored. If the details of the original experience have been lost, we use the schema to fill in the missing details. Because the schema is a record of the common elements of past experiences, it is a good guide to what probably happened. Research indicates that it is usually difficult to distinguish what we actually remember of a past experience and what our memory has reconstructed from the information in the relevant schema. In fact, it is sometimes argued that most memory is a reconstruction rather than an actual recollection of the past.

Different types of memory

There has also been considerable research on distinguishing different types of memory. One distinction that has relevance in the classroom is that between episodic and semantic memory (Tulving, 1993). Episodic memory is memory for the direct personal experience of an event. It contains a record of what was seen, done, or felt at the time. It is always a unique, individual memory. Semantic memory, on the other hand, is memory for the interpretation or understanding of an event. It contains a record of the knowledge and meanings generated by the event, and how the person understood the event and related it to their other knowledge. It is a more abstract memory, related to the knowledge acquired from other people and books. Research suggests that these two types of memory work in different ways. For example, the semantic aspects of an experience may continue to be part of, and change, our knowledge and understanding of the world long after we have forgotten the experience itself (i.e. it has disappeared from episodic memory).

Recently Donald (1991, 1993), using archaeological and historical evidence as well as evidence from contemporary research, has argued that the evolution of human culture has produced four distinct memory systems. These systems have evolved out of the different ways we have learned to interpret and represent experience.

The basic memory system, which humans share with other animals, is episodic. It stores relatively uninterpreted representations of events and experiences. The second memory system, which is uniquely human, is mimetic. It stores representations of behaviours and patterns of activity. The third memory system is linguistic. It involves the internal use of language and imagination, as well as other communally created and shared forms of representation such as artistic symbols. The fourth type of memory has developed from the use of external memory systems such as writing, art, books and information technology. It involves the use of representations that are completely separated from any context, such as computer codes and library catalogues. Donald sees these systems as having their own unique functions, but operating interdependently in the perception, interpretation, and storage of everyday experiences.

Donald's work is significant in that it draws attention to the central role of culture in the creation of memory systems. Each memory system evolved to serve purposes that were important during distinct stages in the evolution of human culture. It is the product of the kinds of tools and forms of human social organisation that were functional at the time, although each new system has added on to, rather than replaced, earlier systems. The result is that we now have a set of memory systems that store and co-ordinate different aspects of our experiences.

3. The design of the research studies

The data used in this booklet comes from a series of studies of pupil learning that Adrienne Alton-Lee and I have carried out as part of the Understanding Learning and Teaching Project at the University of Canterbury. The purpose of the studies was not to investigate memory, but to identify the ways in which pupils learned in typical science and social studies units in upper primary and intermediate school classrooms (see the reports in *set:* Research Information for Teachers, 1987, No.1; 1990, No.2; 1994, No.2). However, as we came to understand the learning process in the classroom, it became clear that we also needed to get a better understanding of how memory affected children's learning.

The design of the studies in the Understanding Learning and Teaching Project followed the same basic format.

1. Planning and test design

First, we approached a teacher (or pair of teachers in the same school) to see if we could record and observe what happened when they were teaching a unit in science or social studies. We talked with the teacher(s) during the initial planning stages of the unit, so that we could create an outcome test that covered everything the teacher(s) intended the pupils to learn, as well as everything else they might learn from resources and other related activities. Table 1 describes the content of the units we observed in each study and how long the units lasted.

TABLE 1: Topics and length of time involved in each unit		
		Length
Topic	Days	Hours
Middle Ages Life and conditions in the Middle Ages in England	21	52.4
New York A study of cultural differences & immigration	5	6.4
Weather Observation and forecasting of weather patterns	8	7.1
Antarctica Working in Antarctica, weather conditions, animals and plants	6	13.4

2. Pre-testing and familiarisation

About two weeks before the unit began, we set up recording equipment in the classroom and familiarised ourselves with the pupils and their routines. About a week before the unit, we administered the outcome test as a pre-test by reading it through with the whole class.

3. Recording and observing

While the unit was in progress, we recorded the pupils' activities using ceiling-mounted miniature video cameras and individually worn miniature microphones. We also made live observations, keeping a running record of every aspect of the children's experiences that we could record.

4. Selection of individual children

Although the equipment was set up to look as though the whole class was being observed and recorded, we made continuous recordings and observations of only four or five selected pupils. These pupils were selected to represent differences in gender, prior achievement, and, where appropriate, ethnic background. Neither the teacher nor the pupils knew who was being observed until the unit and the post-test were completed. The code names and characteristics of these individual children are listed in Table 2.

| | | | | | Interviewed after | | | |
| | | | | Average | 3 | 8 | 12 | Concept |
Study	Student	Gender	Age	percentile[1]	wks	mths	mths	files
Middle Ages	Amy	f	9.9	93	x		x	100
	Kim	m	9.8	30	x		x	99
	Sam	m	9.6	14	x		x	97
New York	Jon	m	11.8	97			x	81
	Mia	f	12.4	96			x	83
	Ann	f	12.5	55			x	82
	Joe	m	12.2	55			x	77
Weather	Rata	f	10.4	68	x			64
	Jan	f	10.4	70	x		x	59
	Pam	f	10.4	21	x		x	68
	Tui	m	10.4	11	x		x	58
Antarctica	Paul	m	12.2	89		x		261
	Jane	f	11.5	83		x		258
	Joy	f	11.10	70		x		267
	Jim	m	11.9	56		x		255
	Teine	f	11.4	34		x		230

TABLE 2: Characteristics of pupils in each study and the timing of interviews

1. Average age-related percentile score on at least three school-administered PAT standardised achievement tests, including reading comprehension.

5. Post-test and interviews

About a week after the unit was completed, the whole class took the outcome test again as a post-test. We then interviewed the selected pupils individually to explore further what they had learned and how they thought they had learned. During the early part of the interview we encouraged pupils to say anything that came to mind — any mental pictures, feelings or thoughts — as they answered the questions. For example:

> Interviewer: Now what I want you to do is, all the thinking that you do, think aloud, so that you can start talking as you're thinking — even if things are jumbled up or whatever — so that I can understand. (Excerpt from interview with Tui)

Typically, the questions asked for each item were:

(a) "How did you learn (know) that?" or "Where did you learn that?"

(b) "Do you remember that coming up in the unit?" or "Was there anything said or done about that in the unit?" or "Where would you have seen (heard about) that?"

(c) "Did you know that before the unit?" or "Did you learn that during the unit?"

We used probing questions, and tried to run the interview on each test question until we had exhausted the pupil's recollections.

6. Long-term post-test and interviews

In three of the studies, we repeated the outcome test and the interviews about eight to twelve months later (see Table 2).

7. Creation of concept files

Once the observations, recordings and interviews were completed and the recordings transcribed and collated, we took each item in the outcome test and put together a file for each pupil. This contained all the data on the pupil's experience that related in any way to the content of that item. Each of these "concept files" contained the detailed story (from our observations and recordings, and from the pupil's own account) of how each item might or might not have been learned, and what the pupil knew before and after the unit and a year later. It was these concept files that provided the data on how each child remembered their classroom learning experiences, and how these memories changed over time.

8. Video-cued interviews

Some of the data used in the last section of this booklet comes from a more recent series of studies in which we have supplemented our standard interviews with video-cued interviews. These involved showing the children video-clips of themselves taking part in activities during the unit. The children were asked to talk about what they were thinking and feeling during the activity shown on the video-clip. This technique provides a more powerful cue for recollecting a past experience than the standard interview.

The use of terms in this booklet

Throughout this booklet I use the terms "recall" and "recollection" more or less interchangeably. They refer to what children say when they are asked to remember what they said or experienced or learned on some previous occasion. These terms need to be distinguished from "recognition", which is what occurs when a child is asked to answer a multiple-choice question and has to identify the correct alternative answer. Although both situations involve memory, recognition is generally considered to be a different — and simpler — kind of task, involving a different memory process.

4. The role of a working memory

In our analysis of the ways in which pupils organised and interpreted their classroom experiences, it became clear that they stored experience in two different kinds of memory: a long-term memory which contained a more or less permanent and well-organised store of past experience, and a working memory which stored experience for about two days. It was in this working memory that new experiences were organised and integrated with other related experiences and with long-term memories. Experiences were forgotten or lost from this working memory if they were not connected to other related experiences within two days (see Figure 1).

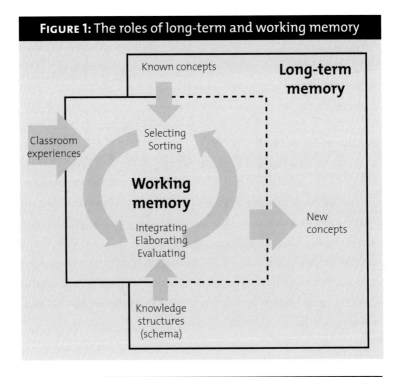

FIGURE 1: The roles of long-term and working memory

Known concepts

Long-term memory

Classroom experiences

Selecting Sorting

Working memory

Integrating Elaborating Evaluating

New concepts

Knowledge structures (schema)

The integration that takes place in working memory is guided by the knowledge structures or schemata that are stored in long-term memory. These schemata determine how a pupil expects experiences and ideas to connect or fit together.

Our continuous observations of individual pupils' experiences show that during the course of a normal school day, each pupil is processing hundreds, if not thousands, of different experiences in working memory at any one time. They are not normally aware of this complex processing, unless the working memory encounters a problem that needs conscious attention. For example, if a pupil experiences something not encountered before, they will feel puzzled or confused, and need to focus on finding some kind of satisfactory connection with previous experience.

5. What do pupils remember?

When we asked pupils to describe what they could remember of their learning experiences, eight to twelve months after each unit, there were occasions when they recalled almost exactly what had happened. For example, when Jan was asked about the liquid in a thermometer, she recalled what the teacher and another pupil had said twelve months earlier.

Interviewer:	Where did you learn that?
Jan:	Last year Mr B said "Does anyone know what mercury is?" and Troy put his hand up and said (correcting herself) Oh no. Mr B said, "What's in a thermometer?" and Troy put his hand up and said it was mercury. And it was right, and since then I have remembered.
Interviewer:	You remember Troy saying that?
Jan:	Yea.
Interviewer:	Isn't that amazing. What did you think at the time, did you think how clever he is or what?... Do you remember that?
Jan:	I thought you have got to be wrong. I thought mercury was a sort of jewel or something like that... Or just a planet.
Interviewer:	So you thought he was wrong?
Jan:	Mm, I thought it was ink or water.

Jan's recollection included not only the detail of what was said, but also what she was thinking at the time. This meant she had stored in memory not only the accepted answer ("mercury"), but her former understanding of the answer ("I thought it was ink or water"), her previous belief about mercury ("a sort of jewel... or just a planet"), and what she felt about the accepted answer.

More often than not, pupils recalled their interpretation of what happened rather than what actually happened. When Pam was asked how a thermometer worked, she recalled her experience of working with thermometers during the weather unit twelve months earlier.

Interviewer: Did you remember thermometers from last year with Mr B?

Pam: Yep, we used to um…

Interviewer: What did you do?

Pam: We used to have thermometers and we used to go outside and if the sun was shining, used to go outside and hold it against the sun and the silver piece would get real hot and um, the ink thing in it, the wee pointer thing would rise to a temperature and then we would take it down, write down what the temperature was. And then Mr B would ask "what temperature was it?" and um, "what do you think — would it be below average or high average" or something like that, 'cause most of us had different temperatures.

Interviewer: Why was that?

Pam: Most people were in different places. They weren't even holding it against the sun. They were not keeping it too far to the sun but back a bit more and people were just holding it there for a while and then they would take it down and it would have different average warmths.

Interviewer: And were you supposed to hold it towards the sun?

Pam: We were just to hold it up and the silver piece had to be down at the bottom and all the heat was going into the thermometer, and the ink stuff was just rising.

Pam's recollection is a summary of what she did ("we used to… go outside and if the sun was shining… hold it against the sun"), what the teacher said ("what temperature was it?"), how she thought thermometers worked ("the ink stuff was just rising"), the lack of agreement among their answers ("most of us had different temperatures"), and why she thought these disagreements occurred. Although it contains some details, her recollection is a summary of what happened over several days and focused on the problem of disagreement among the pupils. The teacher did not actually say, "What temperature was it?" That is Pam's summary or reconstruction of several occasions when the teacher asked questions and gave instructions about measuring and recording the temperature.

As these examples show, pupils can retain the details of experiences in memory for at least twelve months. They can remember both what they learned and many different aspects of the experiences that produced that learning. According to this evidence, memory is unselective, mixing the trivial with the significant, the educationally relevant with the irrelevant, the detail with the generalisation. However, most memories are held together by the pupil's interpretation or understanding of the experience, and it is this interpretation that lasts longest.

6. How do pupils forget?

We expect the passage of time to result in forgetting, first of the details and context of an experience, and later of the more general aspects of the experience. The way in which Amy remembered about the Domesday Book in the unit on the Middle Ages is typical of this forgetting process. During the unit, the teacher talked about William the Conqueror and how he introduced feudal government in England. A description of the Domesday Book came up on the fourth day of the unit.

> Teacher: King William was a shrewd fellow… And he decided that he wasn't going to let anybody get away with not paying taxes. He decided he was going to find out exactly how much land everybody owned, how many buildings were on the land, how many fish ponds, how many rivers, how many mills, how many people, and he was going to collect all this information in a big book. And this book had a special name. And believe it or not, this book is still in existence today. Would anybody like to tell us what the name of this book is? Brian?
>
> Brian: Domesday.
>
> Teacher: Why do you think it's called the Domesday Book? Sue?
>
> Sue: Because it's um…
>
> Teacher: Because it's doom to have to pay taxes?…

When we asked Amy immediately after the unit how she learned about the Domesday Book, she summarised what the teacher had said.

> Amy: Well, we've learned about the Domesday Book and about how William the Conqueror wanted to see how much, see what each man had so much wealth, and things.

Interviewer: Right. How did you learn about it?

Amy: Ms A said that the, when he did go over there [to England] and became King, he wanted the records of each man's wealth. That was called the Domesday Book. That's when I learned about it.

In the interview twelve months later, we again asked Amy how she had learned about the Domesday Book.

Amy: We were taught about it. We had an activity. That was so they knew how much taxes or whatever they were going to... the barons were going to get.

Interviewer: That's great, Amy. Do you remember the activity? Do you remember doing it?

Amy: Yes. I think we did a class one.

The differences between what the teacher actually said and what Amy recalled in the short-term and long-term interviews are consistent with the principle that specific (episodic) details get forgotten first, and are replaced by an interpretation of the experience. With time, this interpretation becomes very general. For example, in the unit on New York, one of the topics was the official seal of New York City. The pupils completed a worksheet that showed the seal and explained what the symbols on it referred to. This was discussed with the whole class. When we asked Ann a year later what she could remember, the only thing that came to mind was "trading".

Ann: I can remember we did something about it but I can't really remember.

Interviewer: OK. Stay with that thought. You "did something about it". Any memories about that?

Ann: Something to do with trading or something, I can't really remember.

Interviewer: Yeah. Was it talked about or was there...?

Ann: I think. Yes, we did talk about it for a while but I can't really remember...

Interviewer:	That's OK. Something to do with trading? Can you follow that up, why you thought it might be something to do with trading?
Ann:	Mm. No, not really.

Gradually, even a generalisation such as "trading" is forgotten and all that is left is a sense of familiarity. Pupils make use of this sense of familiarity, especially when choosing alternatives in multiple-choice questions. During the short-term interview, Amy recalled how she learned that chivalry was a "set of good manners". By the time of the long-term interview, she could remember nothing about chivalry.

Amy (looking at the multiple-choice question):	I don't know. I've heard of it before but I wasn't sure which one. I thought it might of been a "set of good manners"… but I didn't really know.
Interviewer:	Why do you think it might have been a "set of good manners"?
Amy:	Well, I've heard of it before. I thought it was, but I wasn't sure to say definitely it was.
Interviewer:	Did it come up during the Middle Ages unit?
Amy:	I think it came up a bit.

7. Reconstructing and replacing forgotten information

As the details of an experience are forgotten, they can be replaced by the details that a pupil believes should have occurred, based on previous experiences. Knowledge structures, such as schemata, act as "mental templates" which include default information accumulated from previous experiences. During the unit on Antarctica, one of the visiting speakers ('R') talked about sunburn being a problem when the summer sun was shining for 24 hours a day.

> R: ...So that was a bit of a shock to us 'cause we got sunburnt in the middle of the night and all sorts of weird things...

Eight months later, we asked Jim to pick the most significant problem from a list of the problems faced by people working in Antarctica in the summer months. He replied, "Um, serious sunburn from the sunlight reflected off the snow".

> Interviewer: And how did you learn that?
>
> Jim: Um, well, I've heard somewhere, I can't tell you, that um, it shines, the sun shines all day during the summer there, and during the rest of the months it doesn't shine, um, much at all. Um, and, that's in, when it shines there... [it goes] round and round like that, and so on. When it goes round, the sun, which is, the Antarctic's pointing towards the sun for a while, so the sun is always shining on it, so it's, gets pretty hot...
>
> Interviewer: Aha. Well, that's very good. What about the sunburn problem? Did that come up during the unit?
>
> Jim: Um, I can't remember it.

Jim had forgotten what R said about sunburn, but he worked out that sunburn would be a problem if, as he had learned from other sources, the sun shone for 24 hours a day during the summer and would get "pretty hot".

The difference between recollection and reconstruction or deduction is never clear. The evidence suggests that recollection and deduction work in parallel, with one used to check the validity of the other. This is not normally a conscious process. But there is evidence that pupils' minds do not trust spontaneous recollection unless it is consistent with related experiences.

However, deduction can also produce wrong memories. During the short-term interview, Amy recalled how she had learned about the system of "mutual obligations" that characterised the feudal system of government during the Middle Ages.

Amy: Well, we learned about what they [the serfs] had to pay. I don't know which word. To pay hostage or something.

Interviewer: Right, and what did that mean?

Amy: That they had to go and promise they would do certain things for them, the barons, the barons and serfs would go to the King and promise them that they would supply them with knights, people to fight when they needed them. Their service.

Interviewer: Right. And so what, what particular thing helped you to decide that the knights had to look after them [the serfs] by protecting them?

Amy: Well, we, when we learned about that. Ms A did say that they had, that the knights had to promise to protect them.

A year later, Amy remembered that knights had to look after serfs but she had forgotten how the system of mutual obligations was carried out.

Interviewer: How did you know that?

Amy:	We were told the knights had to look after the serfs but I didn't know if it was to supply them with food or to provide them with houses. But as they grow their own food, would of had their own crops, it would be more likely [they had to] provide them with houses.
Interviewer:	Right. Good. Can you remember anything at all about when you were told about the knights looking after the serfs?
Amy:	Not really.

Amy used her belief about how you look after someone ("supply them with food or provide them with houses") and her related knowledge about the lives of the serfs ("would of had their own crops") to deduce, incorrectly, that the knights provided serfs with houses.

Sometimes the errors created by such deductions reflected differences in the cultural beliefs of the pupil and the source of the information. In the unit on Antarctica, both visiting speakers ('R' and 'M') described life at the American base at McMurdo Sound.

| R (talking to class on Day 5 of the unit): | ...McMurdo's not a very beautiful place. It doesn't look very nice and there's lots of rubbish lying around because people don't care about it... all the buildings are a bit grotty. |
| M (talking to class on Day 6 of the unit): | But I hated McMurdo. I thought it was a really grotty place... They simply live there. They want everything, all the comforts of home... And they have this sort of um, recreation room full of video game things... and they had a big shop... At McMurdo a large number of the people there are not volunteers. They are already in the army or the navy or something and they don't want to be there. |

During the long-term interview, most of the pupils recalled that R and M had described McMurdo as a "grotty" place. However, Teine thought that M believed McMurdo was the "nicest base".

| Teine: | She said, um, McMurdo was [the nicest base]. 'Cause they have fish and chips. The games parlour. |

| Interviewer: | The games parlour. Yes. |
| Teine: | And the restaurant. |

Teine recalled M's references to a "recreation room full of video game things" and "a big shop". These must have been associated in Teine's memory with her own experience of a "games parlour". Consequently, she recalled M saying that McMurdo Base was a wonderful place with a restaurant where you could buy fish and chips.

Representations of an experience in memory get stored with the schemata that are used to understand the experiences. Consequently, reconstruction depends on how a pupil understands the original experience. In the unit on the Middle Ages, the teacher spent some time explaining the feudal system of political power and obligations. It first came up when the teacher was describing how William the Conqueror distributed land after he took over as king of England. The teacher explained the system of mutual obligations, and drew a diagram of the feudal political hierarchy on the blackboard. A year later, Kim remembered the diagram sufficiently well to draw it, but misunderstood what it represented.

Kim (pointing to his diagram):	Ah, lords and barons there.
Interviewer:	…What about up there?
Kim:	Oh, probably the king.
Interviewer:	If the king's there, you'd put the…?
Kim:	Well, the church, ah, the church. Yeah, the church there.
Interviewer:	Tell me how you're working that out.
Kim:	Ah, 'cause, the king had… Ah, I can't remember. That's 'cause, I think that king, ah, the church had half, that's a quarter. Knights have a quarter. And so did the lords and barons, I think.
Interviewer:	So you think the system [diagram] is showing how much land they had?
Kim:	Mm.

Because the political system was originally discussed in association with the distribution of land, Kim came to believe that the diagram he recalled was about how the land was divided up.

If significant elements of an experience are forgotten, the reconstruction can be completely wrong. During the unit on the Middle Ages there were several references to the construction of castles. The first occurred during a class discussion about William the Conqueror taking over England.

Teacher: ...William had to settle his army safely in England. He did this by building wooden castles, which could be made very quickly. First he forced the English to build a huge mound of earth... on top was a wooden tower or keep...

Several days later, the class talked about the history of the Tower of London.

Teacher: What was the keep made from? Stan?
Stan: Wood.
Teacher: Why was it made from wood? Mary...?
Mary: Oh, 'cause it was easy to build.
Teacher (later in the discussion): ...But don't forget. It was wood to start off in a hurry, and then it would have been rebuilt... It was started by William the First in 1078. At first there was a wooden castle on a mound of earth.

The important point the teacher made was that there were historical changes in the way castles were built. Subsequently, the pupils studied a worksheet that described the change from wood to stone. They also studied reference books that contained several coloured pictures of castles. When Amy was asked during the short-term interview about medieval castles, her recollection was structured by this idea of historical change and the explanation for it.

Amy:	Well, Ms A told us that the early castles were built of wood because they needed them to get up quickly.
Interviewer:	They needed to get the castles up quickly. Right. And what about stone?
Amy:	I don't think I heard about it. Seen pictures though.
Interviewer:	Right, where would you have seen pictures?
Amy:	This book called *Knights and Castles*... the pictures of the knights coming into the castles and they were brick, grey bricks, stone stuff.

A year later, Amy recalled the pictures of castles but had forgotten about the historical changes in their construction. This led her to conclude that castles were made of "large clay bricks".

Interviewer:	How do you know?
Amy:	I've seen pictures of them before, and they certainly weren't wood and stone and they weren't red bricks and they weren't mud and thatch. They were large clay bricks.
Interviewer:	Right. Where did you see these pictures?
Amy:	On castles, pictures of the rooms of castles.
Interviewer:	Right. That's good. Did Ms A ever talk about what they were actually built of?
Amy:	I think she talked about what the mud and thatch type serfs' type house were made of. I think she talked about that [castles] as well.

This change in Amy's knowledge was a consequence of forgetting about early castles and how they changed. She worked out her answer from her recollection of what castles looked like in pictures.

Visual images and recollections of pictures were often used to deduce or reconstruct information. Sam was explicit about the way he deduced information from the images he reconstructed in his mind.

Interviewer:	About the drawbridge, can you remember how you learned about it?

Sam:	I can see it now. It's a picture in my mind. I don't know. When I don't need it, it just goes away. But when I need it, it just pops in my mind. I can see a drawbridge and a moat and a castle standing right in the middle of it…
Interviewer:	Do you know where the picture comes from?
Sam:	No. I can just see this picture. It's more like a tall castle…

Kim made extensive use of his recollection of a picture of a medieval town square which he had coloured and pasted in his topic book. He also used this picture to work out how fire spread in medieval towns.

Kim:	I can remember, um, in the picture, ah, I could imagine how fire spreading through there, spreading through it. 'Cause the houses was very, very close together. Like it's one big motel about as, um, big as a street. Yeah, not a fence or a garden, just the one big block of houses joined to the next one. No alleyways through.
Interviewer:	Right, and you can remember Ms A saying that.
Kim:	No.
Interviewer:	Well, how else might you have worked that out?
Kim:	Ah, by that picture. (Laughs)

These examples illustrate the ways in which recollection is a problem-solving and interpretive process. The logical processes of inference and deduction are brought to bear on recollections or reconstructions of pictures, diagrams, and narratives, and guided by schema-based expectations about how events and experiences are structured and sequenced.

All these examples highlight the powerful effect that background knowledge has on memory. No matter how the original information is presented, it is the *interpretation* of that information that determines what initially gets stored in memory and how the experience gets recalled or reconstructed at a later date.

8. Memory for classroom activities

Pupils' memories are not designed to focus selectively on the curriculum aspects of their classroom experiences. They appear to recall whatever aspects of their experiences had personal significance for them. For example, when Mia was asked a year later to recall what she had learned about the official seal of New York City, she had only a vague memory of the symbols on the seal, but could recall details of the relevant learning activities.

Mia:	Mm… I can remember learning it, but I just can't remember what it is. Ah, I think it was a transparency Mr B had, but we saw it. I think it's a beaver or otherwise it's a big sea lion. I can't remember though.
Interviewer:	OK. Can you remember anything else about the seal of New York? You remember a transparency?
Mia:	Mm. I think so. That's where it was. Um, we had also a banda [mimeo] sheet I think with it on, for our folders. Think so.
Interviewer:	Can you remember much about your folder?
Mia:	Um, yes. We had lots of [work]sheets of things like the Statue of Liberty. Um. I remember looking, um, no. We had to do a cover. I didn't finish that, 'cause, I got quite cross 'cause Mr B didn't tell us it was due in, and so we had to hand them in and I hadn't done my cover and I was quite cross about that.

It was not unusual for pupils to recall a learning activity without recalling anything they learned during the activity, or even the purpose of the activity.

Pupils' recollections of learning activities faded in the same way as their recollections of curriculum content. In her short-term interview, Amy explained how she learned about the meaning of the word "fallow".

Amy:	Ms A told us about three fields and how one of them was left fallow for a year then another would be left fallow.

Interviewer: Did you have any other activities about that?

Amy: Well, we did have a picture and it had the three fields and one of them was being left fallow and the others had lots growing on them.

A year later, all she could recall was a general description of the learning activities ("being told").

Amy: I remember being told it but I don't know who told me.

Interviewer: You remember being told.

Amy: Yes.

Interviewer: Would that be in the unit or somewhere else?

Amy: I think it would be the unit or activity, I can't really remember now.

Interviewer: But you can remember being told?

Amy: Yes. I can.

As pupils' memories for classroom activities faded, they filled in details from their expectations of what normally happens. In other words, they acquired schemata for classroom activities. When we asked Pam during her long-term interview how she had learned that clouds are made of "white gases", she recalled that the teacher had told her.

Pam: Well, um, Mr C was saying that um, the clouds are made out of white gases and they um, when they um, aw, come in together they get bigger white gases and the clouds sort of move around in different directions and sometimes maybe the white gases can just become small, or they can become medium or big or something and um…

During the weather unit there never was any teacher-led discussion of the composition of clouds. Pam acquired her belief about "white gases" from informal talk with other pupils. However, she had forgotten this and assumed it must have been the teacher who told her. In her experience (i.e. her schemata for classroom activities), the source of knowledge is typically the teacher.

Pupils' memories for classroom activities usually form an integral part of their memories for the curriculum content of the activities. The more they recall the detail of a learning activity, the more likely they are to recall what was learned during the activity. Table 3 shows this relationship in the data of three of our studies.

TABLE 3: Relationship of source of knowledge and answering process to learning outcome at the time of the long-term interview (percentage of items with interview responses)[2]

Recollection of relevant learning activity	Test item outcome[3]		
	Not learned	Learned & forgotten	Learned & remembered
Answer recalled directly from			
Activity outside unit	10.6	12.7	13.4
Activity within unit	11.2	18.2	55.9
Activity not identified	11.2	5.5	16.2
Answer deduced or inferred from			
Activity outside unit	5.0	0	6.1
Activity within unit	6.1	10.9	13.4
Activity not identified	16.2	7.3	7.8
Other			
Guessed or misunderstood	19.6	12.7	1.7
Recalled activity, not content	4.5	18.2	0.6
No recollection of answer	21.8	18.2	1.7
Total number of items with interview responses	179	55	179

---

2. Based on the long-term interviews with the pupils in the Middle Ages study (Kim, Amy, Sam), the New York study (Ann, Mia, Jon, Joe), and the Weather study (Jan, Pam, Tui).

3. 'Learned and forgotten' means that the pupils knew the answer at the time of the short-term test and had forgotten it by the time of the long-term test. 'Learned and remembered' means that the pupils knew the answer on both the short-term and long-term tests.

The Table includes only those items for which pupils were able to recall some aspect of the answer or the relevant learning activity. The answers pupils gave have been divided into three categories: those where the answer was recalled directly; those where the answer was inferred or deduced from related knowledge; and those where the answer was guessed, misunderstood or forgotten. Within the first two categories, the responses have been divided into three further categories: those where the pupil described a learning activity or experience outside the unit; those where they described a learning activity or experience within the unit; and those where they could not recall any relevant learning activity or experience.

As the Table shows, pupils recalled details of the original learning activities or experiences for about 56% of the outcome test answers that they learned from experiences within the unit and could still recall twelve months later (Learned and remembered items, Activity in unit). They could recollect such details for only about 18% of the answers they learned from experiences in the unit but had forgotten twelve months later (Learned and forgotten items, Activity in unit).

When pupils deduced or inferred an answer they were more likely to get the answer right if they could recall the original learning activity (6.1% vs. 10.9% and 13.4%). Conversely, they were less likely to be able to deduce or infer an answer if they could not recall the original learning activity (16.2% vs 7.3% and 7.8%).

It is clear that the more memorable the learning activity itself, the more likely children are to recall or deduce what they learned during the activity.

9. The structure of knowledge in memory

One of the most important functions of working memory is to connect new experiences to existing knowledge. We make sense of new ideas by connecting them to what we already know. As a consequence, new ideas get stored in long-term memory attached to the more general concepts and beliefs (schemata) that were used in making sense of them. When we come to recall these ideas later, the connections with more general concepts and beliefs provide the basis for the memory search process.

These connections can be both helpful and confusing, as the following example illustrates. When we asked Jane in her long-term interview to describe a crevasse, she answered almost immediately.

Jane:	A narrow, deep crack in the ice.
Interviewer:	Right. Now where did you learn that, do you think? I wonder where you learned that.
Jane:	Oh some, I think someone went down, down them.
Interviewer:	Yes. How big are crevasses, what are they like?
Jane:	Um, really deep. And it's kind of all blue, in the middle.
Interviewer:	Yeah. All blue and ice. I wonder where you got that picture from?
Jane:	Probably the slides.

Jane appeared to have a well-established understanding of a crevasse, including details of its appearance, and of how she had learned about it (a visiting speaker had shown slides and told a story about going down a crevasse). However, when we asked her later in the interview to describe a glacier, she expressed confusion. It seemed that her knowledge of a crevasse and her knowledge of a glacier were both attached to her generic schema for ice. When she used this schema to recollect the description of a glacier, she also relocated the description of a crevasse.

Interviewer:	What does a glacier look like, can you imagine one?
Jane:	Um, oh, these two words, one of them's about a ditch, ditch in the ice, that they stand on. And it could either be that or it could be a river of ice, I think. But I don't know what, what the other…
Interviewer:	You can't remember what the other word is.
Jane:	Yeah. Oh yeah, crevasse. That's the one. (Inaudible) The other one's [the glacier's] a river of ice, that's a river of ice.
Interviewer:	So that's a river of ice. Where did you learn about glaciers, do you think?
Jane:	Probably in the unit, yeah.
Interviewer:	Probably in the unit. Yes. If I asked you to draw a picture of a glacier, could you do that, do you think?
Jane:	Um, a little bit. Kind of with all these, um ice going from the start and these bits of ice floating, down. Yeah.

Figure 2 depicts the links between the elements of Jane's understanding of a crevasse and a glacier. Both are attached to her generic schema for ice, and it is this common attachment that is causing the confusion.

Memory search makes use of such links, not only as a map to guide the relocation of information but also as the basis for validating recalled information and inferring missing information.

A number of writers have described recollection as a cyclic or recursive process (e.g. Reisser, 1986). As parts of the original experience are relocated, these act as cues for relocating further aspects of the experience. In the unit on the weather, pupils studied the four major types of cloud. During the long-term interview, Pam could not remember the names of these cloud types. When we asked for the name of the storm cloud, she said she didn't know.

Pam:	I don't know… One of them is like a pig's tail anyway. Think it's…

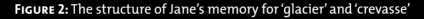

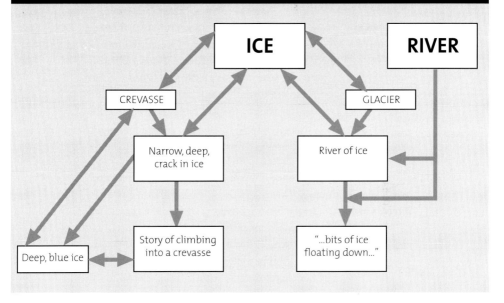

FIGURE 2: The structure of Jane's memory for 'glacier' and 'crevasse'

Interviewer: Which one do you think will be the storm cloud? Did you put down "I don't know" in the test?

Pam: Yep. I put "I don't know" for all of them, apart from that one there, because I couldn't remember any of them. I think for a storm cloud, is nimbus.

Interviewer: Now what makes you think that?

Pam: We talked about [it] last (laugh), last year, um, when we went outside and had our [wind] vanes and that. We used to sit down on the grass and Mr C would tell us, "This one here is such and such and it's like a pig's tail, and this one's such and such, lays out straight." The one that lays out straight I'm sure is stratus or whatever.

Pam went on to name the other major cloud types, and said she used to look them up in the encyclopaedia. The interviewer asked her why she had said in the test that she could not remember them.

Interviewer:	You said the other day you put "I don't know", "I don't know"… You just told me a storm cloud is nimbus, flat layer cloud is stratus, a tail cloud is cirrus and a big white fluffy cloud is cumulus, with no hesitation at all! How do you think you have just done that…?
Pam:	Probably looking at the [test] sheet again or it could have just clicked in my mind that I just remembered. It's hard since it was last year, it's hard to remember things.
Interviewer:	You remember Mr B talking about those clouds. Do you remember any pictures of them?
Pam:	He drew some on the blackboard, all red (laugh). He didn't do them in white, he did them all red… He did pigs' tails, big fluffy one, feathery tailed one, flat layers and a stormy one.
Interviewer:	Did you do any drawings?
Pam:	We had to do them on a piece of paper and hand them in to Mr C… We had to do, it was on a red piece of paper but we had to do it in pencil and um, we got a piece of, um, paper and Mr C did them, we had to do them sort of like that, except I didn't know. And we had to do the clouds, remember what the clouds were 'cause he would rub it [the clouds] off the board. But he would leave the names. We had to sort of remember what the clouds were.

It is clear that once Pam started to recall the original learning experiences ("when we went outside and had our [wind] vanes and that…"), this cued the recollection of both the names of the cloud types and details of the original learning experiences.

This memory search process occurs automatically, below the level of consciousness. Evidence for the way it works emerges only when it runs into difficulties and some kind of conscious strategy or focused effort is required. One such difficulty occurs when the search produces two answers. This happened when we asked Sam to name the stocks in a picture of a medieval village square.

Sam: A guillotine or the stocks. One of those two.
Interviewer: Well, why do you think it's a guillotine?
Sam: I don't know. A guillotine sounds like a word where
                     they go to. The stocks is, ah, where they go, too. Yeah,
                     I think it may be the stocks. But I think it must be the
                     stocks, but if I am wrong it's the guillotine. It just
                     popped into my mind. Guillotine and stocks. They are
                     both having a fight now. They are having a fight over
                     which one is the right name.

When the search produces alternative answers, the person looks for additional evidence that might resolve the dilemma. In this case, Sam tried the strategy of using the words in an appropriate sentence ("the guillotine is where they go to", "the stocks is where they go"), but both seemed to fit equally well. As Sam said, the alternatives compete ("they are having a fight") until evidence is found to support one or the other.

Some information cannot be logically connected to prior knowledge or beliefs. The names of things, for example, are usually arbitrary and difficult to recall. That "tip of the tongue" feeling is the frustration of knowing we know something without being able to recall it. Jane had this experience when she tried to remember the name of a lake in Antarctica. Both visiting speakers in the unit on Antarctica had shown pictures of the lake and talked about visiting it. The second speaker described the area in some detail, and gave an explicit account of the traditional practice of swimming in the lake with no clothes on. During the talk Jane took notes, and later wrote a report that included the sentence: "M had a swim in Lake Vanda". During the interview eight months later, Jane recalled much of what M had said, but not the name of the lake.

Jane:	Oh yeah, there was this um… lake that um I think… I don't think it iced over, I'm not quite sure… and they had to go swimming in it to get a badge thing.
Interviewer:	Who did that?
Jane:	Um, probably, I think M did.
Interviewer:	Right. Right. Do you remember what it was called, the name of the lake?
Jane:	Mm. No. I think it had um, rocks, quite a few round it.
Interviewer:	It had rocks around it?
Jane:	Yeah.
Interviewer:	So do you have a picture in your mind of it, do you think?
Jane:	A little bit.
Interviewer:	A little bit. So you must have seen a picture of it, perhaps.
Jane:	Yeah.

Later, when talking about M's work in Antarctica, Jane again recalled the swim in the lake.

Jane:	Yeah. And she went to that lake (laugh), for a swim.
Interviewer:	For a swim. That lake for a swim?
Jane:	Yeah.
Interviewer:	Remember the name of the lake?
Jane:	No (laugh). She went, um, well on an expedition.

However, when Jane later saw the name of the lake in the test booklet, she instantly recognised it.

Jane:	And, Lake Vanda!
Interviewer:	You remember Lake Vanda?

Jane:	Aha. It's that lake where she went swimming, I think…
Interviewer:	Right. Do you remember seeing a picture of it?
Jane:	Yeah I think so. Sort of had all these stones I think.

With arbitrary knowledge such as names, the processes of memory search and deduction cannot support each other. Recall is completely dependent on relocating the original experience, and when that fails nothing can be reconstructed. Even though Jane knew a lot about Lake Vanda, it was not until she actually saw the name that she made the connection.

These three examples (Jane and glaciers, Pam and types of cloud, Jane and Lake Vanda) make it clear that the ability of pupils to give correct answers on tests is not dependent just on what they know and have learned. It is also dependent on an effective memory search process, which in turn depends on the way knowledge is organised (interconnected) in memory.

10. Acquiring a memory: Piaget and Vygotsky

Both Piaget and Vygotsky have argued that the way our minds (including our memories) work is the result of internalising our interactions with the physical and social world (see, for example, Piaget, 1962, 1978; Vygotsky, 1978). On the basis of this view, it seems likely that the way pupils remember their classroom experiences is the result of the way their memories get used and shaped during daily classroom activities. In the course of most school days, pupils are constantly engaged in recollecting what they have done and learned in previous hours, days and weeks.

Piaget has argued that internalisation is the result of increasing expertise in an activity. When a child first undertakes a new activity, she is almost completely dependent on external feedback. The process is one of trial and error as the child tentatively tries out initial actions and experiences the consequences. For example, if a child is learning how to use a new construction toy and tries to build a model house, there will be several attempts to put the parts together in a way that works. Different combinations will fall over until the child discovers a combination that results in a building that does not fall down. Or if a child is learning how to make friends with another child, there will be several attempts at approaching potential new friends until a way is discovered that produces the desired reactions. During this stage, play is often the context for trying alternative versions of the same behaviours and noticing variations in their effects.

Gradually, as a child becomes more familiar with an activity, she can anticipate the likely consequences of each of the behaviours that make up the activity. The child builds up an increasingly elaborate map of the activity in memory (e.g. of alternative ways of carrying it out, of outcomes, and of different contexts). Imaginative play may accompany this stage as the child learns the patterns of behaviours and their consequences and is able to separate the activity from its original purpose and context. For example, the child may enact meetings between dolls, replaying in varying sequences and combinations remembered reactions to her own attempts to engage the friendship of other children. In this way, the child learns to carry out the activity as an integrated system of behaviours (or schema) in a variety of make-believe and real contexts.

As this process occurs, the child becomes capable of carrying out the activity in her head, and can experiment with the effects of alternative behaviours without needing to try them out in the real world. The child is now capable of planning the activity, and control of what happens has been transferred from the outside world into the child's mind. This internal planning and experimenting is what we call thinking.

For Vygotsky the process is similar in many respects. The important difference is that Vygotsky focused on the internalisation of the social world rather than the physical world. He understood that much of children's knowledge comes from the experience of others, rather than their own direct experience of the world. Consequently, he focused on the way children acquire patterns of thinking and knowing from those already established in their culture and embodied in its language, customs and tools. Children learn to think by interacting with more mature members of the society and internalising the language, customs and tools they use. For example, the behaviour of young children is managed by adults telling them what to do, and praising them for following — or admonishing them for not following — their instructions. Through this interaction with adults, children learn the language of control. In imaginative play, children practise the roles of both adult and child. By internalising the role and language of the adult, children acquire self-control, at first through talking aloud to themselves, telling themselves what to do, and ultimately through internal self-instructions.

In explaining how thinking and memory develop, Piaget and Vygotsky focus on the routine activities that make up our daily lives and become the unconscious habits of mind. By contrast, some claim that thinking is a natural function of the brain which develops according to genetic instructions as the brain matures. Another view is that thinking and remembering skills can be taught by training children to teach themselves how to think and remember.

The theories of Piaget and Vygotsky suggest that school experience plays an important role in the development of children's thinking and memory. As children become expert in the routine activities of the classroom, internalising the roles of both teacher and pupil, they acquire the school's ways of interpreting and remembering their experiences. In other words, the child's mind internalises the culture of the classroom.

11. Activities that shape memory in the classroom

In order to understand how pupils' memories are shaped by their classroom experiences, we need to identify the classroom routines that involve the use of memory. What is it that children are doing on a daily basis that requires them to use their memories?

The following example illustrates the way one teacher engaged her pupils in memory activities, although like most teachers she was not aware she was doing so. Her intention was to set up a series of activities that would help the children get the most benefit from a talk by a visiting speaker.

The speaker ('R') came into the classroom one morning and talked about her time in Antarctica as a volunteer worker. In the afternoon, the teacher asked the children to work in pairs and identify the "best or most interesting" aspects of R's talk.

> Teacher: Right. With the person next to you, I want you to remember way back to this morning, way back to this morning and to have a little discussion about R's talk and to tell each other what you thought the best part or most interesting part was for you. OK? Just with the person next to you.

The teacher wanted this brainstorming activity to provide the basis for a whole class discussion. Working in pairs, the children could develop each other's ideas without having to risk speaking unprepared before the whole class. After about four minutes, the teacher started the whole class discussion.

> Teacher: And I want you just to tell me something that you remembered really well, something that was interesting to you or just a comment in general about the talk that R gave this morning.

During this discussion the teacher progressively shaped the way the children recalled R's talk. For example, in the earlier brainstorming session Paul and Cory had discussed the things they had found most interesting.

Paul: The slides.
Cory: The most interesting part was the slides?
Paul: Yeah. I reckon the slides were the best.
Cory: And how heavy and thick the clothes were…

When the class discussion began, Paul was the first to be asked for his contribution. He repeated (as he thought he was supposed to) what he had said to Cory. But this was not what the teacher wanted.

Paul: Um, I liked the slides best.
Teacher: OK then. What particular slide or slides stood out in your memory?
Paul: Um… One with the helicopter on the ice.
Teacher: OK. Why did that stand out?
Paul: Um, I dunno! It just did.
Teacher: Well, what was the helicopter doing on the ice?
Paul: Um, it just landed there.
Teacher: Well, what did she say about it though? What was the interesting thing that she said about it?
Paul: Um, it was a heavy one and the guy got out and checked the ice with his axe afterwards.
Teacher: Afterwards. OK. It'd be too bad if the helicopter went straight through, wouldn't it?

Through further questioning, the teacher helped Paul to elaborate his recall. She progressively modelled, with his assistance, recall of an entire episode, including the reasons for it. The other children appear to have noted this model and changed their recall accordingly. For example, during the brainstorm, Jane had recalled penguins and skiing.

Jane: Well, the most interesting thing… I liked when she saw the penguins… And that would have been fun going skiing, on the back [of a truck].

Tilly:	Yeah.
Jane:	That sounds (inaudible).
Tilly:	It sounds like she had a really good time, 'cause she said it was absolutely fun…

In the class discussion, however, Jane's response was closer to what she thought was the teacher's idea of significant information.

Jane:	I, um, I liked the um… I was surprised 'cause I asked her how many mountains there was and she said millions and millions of mountains.
Teacher:	(laughs)
Jane:	I liked the view from the top of the mountain looking over.
Teacher:	OK. What mountain was it?
Girl:	Erebus.
Jane:	Yeah.

As each child contributed to the discussion, the teacher helped them to elaborate their recall by adding reasons, explanations, and additional details. Towards the end of the discussion, the teacher took the process further and modelled the memory search process itself.

Joy:	…Um, I liked the snow mound and seeing the old clothes and things.
Teacher:	Right. The old clothes… What hut was that in? Can you remember?
Several pupils:	Scott.
Teacher:	Scott. Right. It was in Scott's hut. Who else was the other explorer's hut that they had a look in?
Several pupils:	Shackleton.
Teacher:	Right. And another one, was there?
Several pupils:	McMurdo.
Girl:	No. That's a base.
Girl:	Amundsen.
Teacher:	Amundsen they *didn't* have.
Maude:	They didn't have that. They only had two [huts].
Leigh:	They went to three places.

Teacher:	They did go to three places too. You're right. They went back to Scott Base, I think it was.
Maude:	No. No. They went to the Dry Valley.
Leigh:	Yeah, they went to the Dry Valley…
Teacher:	That's it! Dry Valley, Shackleton's hut and Scott's hut. If I remember rightly. But I'll check that anyway and see…

In this excerpt, the teacher and the children worked together to construct a summary account of R's visit to Antarctica. The teacher supported the children as they corrected one another's recall. She made use of a summary framework suggested by a pupil ("they went to three places"), both to evaluate the completeness of their recall and to act as a cue to search for the third place ("the Dry Valley"). She ended by summarising the list of places R had visited ("Dry Valley, Shackleton's hut and Scott's hut"), and suggested that this was a vulnerable memory activity which needed to be verified ("If I remember rightly. But I'll check that anyway and see").

The teacher followed up this activity by asking the children to write a report on what R had said. To make it more challenging, she suggested that they write it as a newspaper report. Each child interpreted this task differently. Jane wrote a report that was close in style (genre) to an actual newspaper report.

…*She travelled over on a Hercules. The aeroplane landed on the ice with sea underneath it. She stayed at Scott Base. R went with four others…*

Joy wrote a report based on the model the teacher had established during the class discussion. It was about what she found interesting and surprising.

…*some interesting facts and things I really liked were that it was really interesting to see inside Shackleton's hut and see all the old clothes…*

Teine interpreted the task as having to write about something controversial, so she used an argumentative style.

…On the plane which R described as a squashing experience because R told us that your knees would nearly touch the person sitting opposite you. The plane was a cargo ship. I suggest that's why they got squashed…

Jim, who had difficulties with spelling, focused on the appearance of his report. After spending some time deciding on a title and announcing it to all those around him ("Skinny-dipping in Antarctica"), he spent the rest of the time measuring and ruling columns on his page so that he could set out his report in a three-column format. Unfortunately, there was no time left for him to write more than the heading and a single phrase ("R has resenly been to Antarctica so R").

The newspaper report format required the children to use their memory selectively. In the class discussion, they had been asked to give an elaborated account of some aspect of R's talk. The newspaper report required another kind of account, and another way of using their recall. None of the reports contained everything the children remembered about R's talk. Paul, for example, began by reading a list of relevant words the teacher had written on the board. He then looked at the many pictures of Antarctica on the classroom walls, and sat thinking and occasionally talking to himself, before beginning to write a long report.

On the morning of Thursday 22ⁿᵈ August, R came to talk to us.
First she started to talk to us and show us slides…

These activities are typical of the ways in which teachers require pupils to use their memories. At no point did the teacher ask the children to memorise what R had said, but there was always an expectation that they would discuss what she had said and perhaps write a report. Repeated often enough, this pattern of activity would require children to develop a working memory for holding activities in mind for periods of several hours or days, without engaging in specific memorisation. Without this working memory, children risk being embarrassed during class discussions and unable to carry out required tasks.

The way the teacher managed the class discussion and structured the subsequent report developed the children's expectations that their knowledge should be elaborated with reasons and implications, and that they should be able to recall selectively what they knew in order to carry out the required tasks. Developing these ways of organising memory and recall is part of becoming an "expert" in classroom routines.

12. What this means for teaching

The results of our studies point to a number of different ways in which we should be thinking about classroom activities, and about their effects on children's learning and especially on the development of their minds.

1. The accessibility of knowledge

Perhaps the most important and obvious of our findings is that pupils cannot always recall what they know. Knowing something and remembering it are not the same thing. It is not enough for a child to have learned something. That learning must be readily accessible if it is to be useful and shape the way the child perceives and interprets new experiences. This means that teachers need to shape the learning process so that new experiences are extensively interconnected with other related experiences and knowledge.

Recent research on the neurophysiology of the brain indicates that knowledge stored in memory is involved not only in interpreting new experiences but also in helping the brain to anticipate what is likely to happen next. This means that our minds are primed to see what we expect to see (McCrone, 1999). When a child has a wide range of readily accessible background knowledge, their mind is automatically primed to recognise and relate to a greater variety of different aspects of a new experience.

2. Focusing the experience of pupils

We also found that pupils' memories for classroom learning activities are as much about the physical and social aspects of those activities as they are about the curriculum. Pupils learn and remember what they do. It is easy to assume that learning activities are simply the vehicle for learning the curriculum. For the pupils, however, the activities themselves are central. In recent studies, when we asked pupils to talk about their classroom experiences as they watched video recordings of themselves, it was clear that negotiating the physical and social complexities of tasks was their predominant concern. From their point of view, life in the classroom is less about learning the curriculum and more about lending erasers and borrowing felt-tip pens, finding out how much to write and how to set it out, negotiating relationships with other pupils, getting things finished before the bell, finding work that has been lost, and generally following the myriad rules that surround being a well-behaved or unobtrusive pupil.

This arises partly from a teacher's need to put class management before learning. As a consequence, we talk a lot about the physical aspects of tasks and little, if anything, about the learning and thinking processes that the tasks are intended to promote. This suggests that we need to do two things. First, we should try to make memory for the physical aspects of classroom activities supplement and support the intended curriculum outcomes. This means creating tasks in which the process is as important as the product. For example, if the task requires writing, then the writing itself should engage the pupil in planning, organising, selecting, summarising, and explaining, rather than just recording or reporting.

Second, we need to develop with pupils the language for talking about our thinking processes. If learning, remembering and thinking processes are to be the focus of an activity, then children need to learn how to talk about these processes. As well as telling them how many words to write, how to set out their topic books, and how to record their results, we need to explain to them what we expect will be going on in their minds during the activity. Pupils need to internalise language that describes the processes of the mind in order to learn how to manage their own learning, remembering and thinking.

3. Managing social processes

The same applies to the social interaction involved in class activities. Children remember the roles they play. Being liked or humiliated, being included or ignored, being respected or put down, are all part of the content of what is learned. When pupils are working together inclusively and co-operatively, they are not merely learning social skills. Their social experiences are stored as integral parts of the scientific concept or mathematical procedure they are supposed to be learning. The personal and social quality of the classroom environment, its culture and routines, are the real curriculum. As Wertsch, Tulviste, and Hagstrom put it: "...the nature of individuals' mental functioning can be understood only by beginning with a consideration of the social system in which it exists" (1993, p.336).

Related to this is the extent to which pupils come to trust their own remembering and thinking processes. There are pupils who come to believe, from repeated classroom experiences, that what they remember must be wrong in some way. There are pupils who do not believe they know anything of value and hence do not bother to search memory. Memory search is cued by the initial belief that memory is worth searching. We do not try to remember things we know we have not experienced or do not believe we could remember. Making an accurate judgement about what is in memory depends on how well our memories are organised. There is no space here to explore the beliefs that children have about their memories, and how these are shaped. But it is important to note that children's respect or lack of respect for each other and each other's contributions to classroom activities has a powerful effect on the development of their ability to use their memories.

4. Memory as a problem-solving process

Another important finding relates to the way knowledge is organised in memory. Two processes are involved in recall: relocating the experiences that are stored in memory, and reconstructing experiences. These processes are interdependent, and memory works best when both work in parallel. Successful recollection and reconstruction depends on the way memory is organised. A coherent, consistent, and logical system of connections provides a kind of map which makes recollection and reconstruction more consistent and effective. This means that experiences that are well understood, in the sense that the child has thought about the reasons and implications associated with the experience, are much more likely to be readily available in memory. There are more interconnections with other knowledge, and better structures for finding the way around these interconnections. For example, if pupils in a classroom learn to ask "why" as a matter of habit, their working memories will be shaped to deal with experience in more efficient and complex ways. Habitually, unconsciously, asking "why" is one way of producing elaborately interconnected knowledge.

5. Expanding working memory

A child's ability to use and learn from experience depends on their having a working memory that automatically and unconsciously connects and organises experience in appropriate ways. How working memory functions depends on the "habits of mind" a pupil acquires from participating in classroom activities. Pupils who expect they will need to recall experiences two or three days after they occur are likely to develop working memories that store information in a readily available form for that length of time. The activity of constantly referring back to previous experiences builds up the range of experience that pupils will automatically bring to mind when dealing with new experiences.

All of these topics suggest that we need to rethink our understanding of how schools shape children's minds. Classrooms are places where pupils' memories and thought processes are constantly being used in particular ways. As a result, these processes are internalised as habits of mind. This is different from teaching specific memory or thinking skills. Such skills can be taught, and we usually teach them in the same way we teach mathematical or writing skills. But specifically taught memory and thinking skills get used only when the pupil remembers to use them. They will never become an essential part of the way a pupil's mind works until they become part of the pervasive culture of the classroom, and are internalised through habitual use. They become the mechanisms for processing the hundreds, if not thousands, of experiences that working memory is constantly dealing with below the level of consciousness. Internalisation, of the kind described by Piaget and Vygotsky, is what drives the development of mind.

Consequently, pupils who understand and accept the goals and routines that make up a classroom activity are more likely to participate fully in the activity, and hence to acquire the ways of thinking and remembering embedded in the activity. They develop minds that unconsciously conform to the way schools work. Conversely, pupils who do not participate fully do not develop minds that cope easily with classroom tasks. As a result, classroom activities present them with problems they are ill-equipped to solve.

This booklet has examined the way pupils remember their classroom experiences. As the opening quotation from Katherine Nelson indicated, memory is central to almost all cognitive processes. Enhancing the way pupils organise and structure their knowledge affects not only what they know and how they use what they know, but also those underlying cognitive processes that ultimately determine their level of intelligence.

Further reading

More extensive material on our research on memory can be found in:

Graham Nuthall (1999). The anatomy of memory in the classroom: Understanding how students acquire memory processes from classroom activities in science and social studies units. *American Educational Research Journal, 36* (2).

Graham Nuthall (2000). The role of memory in the acquisition and retention of knowledge in science and social studies units. *Cognition & Instruction, 18* (1), 83-139.

An earlier account of our research on classroom learning can be found in:

Graham Nuthall & Adrienne Alton-Lee (1994). How pupils learn. *set No.2,* Item 3 (Wellington: NZCER).

More recent accounts of our research on classroom learning can be found in:

Graham Nuthall (1998). Understanding student thinking and learning in classrooms. In B. J. Biddle, T. L. Good, & I. F. Goodson (Eds.) *The International Handbook of Teachers and Teaching* (pp.681-768). Dordrecht: Kluwer Academic Publishers.

Graham Nuthall (1999). The way students learn: Acquiring knowledge from an integrated science and social studies unit. *The Elementary School Journal, 99* (4), 303–341.

Graham Nuthall (1999). Learning how to learn: The evolution of students' minds through the social processes and culture of the classroom. *International Journal of Educational Research, 31* (3), 139–256.

References

Alton-Lee, A. G., Nuthall, G. A., & Patrick, J. (1987). Take your brown hand off my book. *set No.1*, Item 8 (Wellington: NZCER).

Alton-Lee, A. G., Densem, P., & Nuthall, G. (1990). "I only think of men... I don't think of the women". *set No.2*, Item 16 (Wellington: NZCER).

Donald, M. (1991). *Origins of the human mind: Three stages in the evolution of culture and cognition.* Cambridge, MA: Harvard University Press.

Donald. M. (1993). Précis of: Origins of the human mind: Three stages in the evolution of culture and cognition. *Behavioral and Brain Sciences, 16,* 737-791.

Fivush, R. (1991). The social construction of personal narratives. *Merrill-Palmer Quarterly, 37,* 59-82.

Fivush, R., Haden, C., & Adam, S. (1995). Structure and coherence of preschoolers' personal narratives over time: Implications for childhood amnesia. *Journal of Experimental Child Psychology, 60,* 32-56.

Hudson, J. A. (1990). The emergence of autobiographic memory in mother-child conversation. In R. Fivush & J. A. Hudson (Eds.) *Knowing and remembering in young children* (pp.166-196). New York: Cambridge University Press.

Kreutzer, M. A., Leonard, C., & Flavell, J. H. (1975). An interview study of children's knowledge about memory. *Monographs of the Society for Research in Child Development, 40* (1) (Serial no.159).

McCrone, J. (1999). *Going inside: A tour round a single moment of consciousness.* London: Faber & Faber.

Morrison, F. J., Smith, L., & Dow-Ehrensberger, M. (1995). Education and cognitive development: A natural experiment. *Developmental Psychology, 31,* 789-799.

Neisser, U. (1989). Domains of memory. In P. R. Soloman, G. R. Goethals, C. M. Kelley, & B. R. Stephens (Eds.) *Memory: Interdisciplinary Approaches* (pp.67-83). New York: Springer Verlag.

Nelson, K. (1993). The psychological and social origins of autobiographical memory. *Psychological Science, 4,* 7-14.

Nelson, K. (1996). *Language in cognitive development: The emergence of the mediated mind.* New York: Cambridge University Press.

Piaget, J. (1962). *Play, dreams, and imitation in childhood.* New York: Norton.

Piaget, J. (1978). *Success and understanding.* London: Routledge & Kegan Paul.

Reisser, B. J. (1986). The encoding and retrieval of memories of real world experiences. In J. A. Galambos, R. P. Abelson, & J. B. Black (Eds.) *Knowledge structures* (pp.71-99). Hillsdale, NJ: Lawrence Erlbaum Associates.

Sharp, D., Cole, M., & Lave, J. (1979). Education and cognitive development: The evidence from experimental research. *Monographs of the Society for Research in Child Development, 38* (5, No.152).

Tulving, E. (1993). What is episodic memory? *Current Directions in Psychological Science, 2,* 67-70.

Vygotsky, L. S. (1978). *Mind in society: The development of higher psychological processes.* (M. Cole, V. John-Steiner, S. Scribner, & E. Souberman, Eds.) Cambridge, MA: Harvard University Press.

Wertsch, J. V., Tulviste, P., & Hagstrom, F. (1993). A sociocultural approach to agency. In E. A. Forman, N. Minick, & C. A. Stone (Eds.) *Contexts for learning: Sociocultural dynamics in children's development* (pp.336-356). New York: Oxford University Press.